dedicated to all those who are lost but never forgotten.

I am not, nor do I claim to be a medical professional.
If you are having suicidal thoughts, please use these
resources:

National Suicide Hotline: 1-800-273-8255
Crisis Textline: text "HOME" to 741741
Online Crisis Chat: https://suicidepreventionlifeline.org/
chat/

THE
GRIEF
WORKBOOK

this workbook belongs to:

_____

Grief Workbook

*what's inside this workbook,
my love:*

Grief Workbook

how to use this workbook

WHAT TO EXPECT

In this workbook, you will first harness a deep understanding of Grief as a concept. After learning more about the 7 phases of grief, you will move through each phase using journaling prompts, somatic exercises, and actionable tools.

WHAT YOU WILL LEARN

- ❖ The 7 phases of grief,

- ❖ What the experience of each phase may feel like

- ❖ Goal of each phase

- ❖ Challenges of each phase

HOW TO USE THE EXERCISES

You will essentially "move through" each phase of grief using journaling prompts, somatic activities, and actionable tools.

Choose ONE area of grief in your life--it can be a current grief or past grief, this workbook is supportive for both.

Each exercise will have clear instructions for how to engage with that particular grief phase.

Grief Workbook

how to use this workbook

RACHEL'S RECOMMENDATION REMINDERS

You can use the exercises in this workbook as many times as you need, and for as many experiences of grief as you desire.

I invite you to choose ONE area of grief to focus on at a time, and move fully through the workbook before choosing a new experience.

There is no timeframe for completing this workbook--I invite you to take your time and go slow.

My recommendation, if you are unsure how long to spend on each phase, is focusing on one area of grief per week. You can either repeat the exercises from one phase multiple times during one week, or etake a full week to slowly move through the exercise associated with each phase.

On Grief:

Grief is messy. It hits us all at once, or not at all. Each phase can show up more than once, and all out of order. This workbook aims to honor the non-linear-ness of grief, the same way my work always honors the fluid, flexible, and unpredictable-ness that is life.

SEVEN PHASES OF GRIEF
Background & Overview

TRADITIONAL 5 STAGES OF GRIEF

Traditionally, we understand the process of grief through the "5 Stages of Grief Model," which was originally developed by Elizabeth Kubler-Ross.

Kubler-Ross actually developed these stages to help terminally ill patients come to terms with their diagnoses and ultimate fate with death--not for people to grief the loss of someone or something the way we now apply the concepts.

Still, these stages have created a framework for many that feels comforting: it is a process we can name, identify with, and use as a benchmark for where we stand in the painful journey of moving through grief.

NEWER MODELS; 7 STAGES

While Kubler-Ross describes 5 Stages of Grief (Denial, Anger, Bargaining, Depression, Acceptance), there are newer models that have 7 stages that align more with the process of grieving more complex, nuanced, or traumatic losses.

THIS WORKBOOK: 7 PHASES

This workbook includes those 7 stages, which I am referring to as "phases" because more often than not, we experience grief in cyclical waves that don't always follow a sequential, step-by-step process.

SEVEN PHASES OF GRIEF

The Seven Phases

Shock & Denial

Pain & Guilt

Anger & Bargaining

Depression

The Upward Turn

Reconstruction & Working Through

Acceptance & Hope

*each phase will be explained in the
exercises to follow.*

MOVING THROUGH

Exercises, Somatic Activities, &
Action Items for Each Phase

The next section of this workbook is dedicated to working through each phase listed above.

Each phase includes a description of the experience, goal, and challenge of each phase. You will be given journaling prompts, somatic exercises, and action items for each phase.

Loving Reminders When Grieving:

In grieving any loss, it is important to remember these stages rise and fall, move backwards and forwards, jump ahead and go backwards, and do not move in perfect linear fashion.

If you find yourself in bargaining, and the next day returning to denial, it is completely normal. Grief does not follow this model: this model was made to help us name and understand the process, even though it's not a perfect system.

Allow yourself permission to be in whatever stage you are in, and honor that you may revert to a previous stage, jump ahead, or skip one entirely. This is not bad, wrong, good, or right. It simply is.

PHASE ONE
Shock & Denial

DATE:

This week, I'd like you to take some time to journal through the first stage of grief: "Shock/Denial."

You can do this all at once, more than once, or in chunks throughout the week.

Additionally, I will invite you to do some somatic (physi cal) practices related to this journaling exercise, which are below the journaling prompts.

NOTE: Please make sure you are in a safe, quiet, comfortable space (mentally and physically) when beginning this. You can set up a cozy nook in your room, light a candle, or play soft music. Make sure you won't be distracted or interrupted (avoid public places and try to turn your phone off). This practice may bring up a lot physically and emotionally, and it's important to take good care of yourself before, during, and after.

ABOUT
Shock & Denial

EXPERIENCE

Often, this is the most traumatic and complicated phase to move through. When we experience shock, our brain can sometimes move into Fight/ Flight/Freeze, creating a trigger reaction of numbness, shutting down, inability to contextualize or place the experience into place, time, or memory, and complex processing.

CHALLENGE

Staying in the body, staying present, incorporating experience into memory

GOAL

Get grounded, integrate the reality into memory, feel the shock and denial in the body, acknowledge the shock and allow for the emotions to be felt

Note: Often, shock and denial are revisited time and time again during the grief process, as each new emotion is a reminder of the bizarre and unfathomable loss that shakes us to our core.

JOURNALING PROMPTS
Shock & Denial

What is the event, experience, or loss I am grieving and working through for this exercise? *Describe it in as much detail as you are able to, recalling the date, weather, where you were, what you heard, smelled...try to incorporate in your journaling a full story that encompasses all the senses surrounding the event/how you learned of the event.*

When I first heard about/learned of/experienced the event, what were my thoughts?

When I first heard about/learned of/experienced the event, what happened in my body?

JOURNALING PROMPTS
Shock & Denial

When I first heard about/learned of/experienced the event, what were my emotions?

What shocked me about this event? How long did the shock last? Am I still in shock about anything?

Where do I feel shock in my body?

In what ways did I deny the reality of what happened?

JOURNALING PROMPTS
Shock & Denial

How did my denial manifest physically?

What am I still in denial about?

What does denial feel like in my body? Where do I feel it?

JOURNALING PROMPTS
Shock & Denial

What makes it hard to integrate this experience into reality?

What would it mean if this was really real?

What do I need to integrate this experience into reality and as something that has occurred in the past?

SOMATIC ACTIVITIES
Shock & Denial

IDENTIFY: Once you have moved through the journaling prompts, make a brief list of the places you identified feeling shock and denial in your body below:

ACTIVITY: Find a comfortable seated position, and place one hand over the body part you have identified, and another over your heart. You can close your eyes or keep them open.

Gently massage, rub in circles, or use two fingers to "tap" the identified, while repeating these mantras to yourself:

"I am shocked."
"I am in shock."
"I cannot believe this is happening."
"This can't be real."

Repeat any of them as many times as you need until you begin to physically and emotionally experience the shock and denial.

Slowly invite yourself out of the practice, repeating this for any physical area you identified in your original list, and as many times as you wish throughout the week.

SOMATIC ACTIVITIES
Shock & Denial

Then, repeating the physical movements, begin saying these mantras:

"This was a shocking experience."
"My shock is completely warranted."
"This is hard to fathom."
"Of course it's hard to believe."

Repeat any of them as many times as you need until you begin to physically and emotionally expereince the shock and denial.

Then, repeating the physical movements, begin saying these mantras:

"I have permission to feel this shock for as long as I need to."
"I have permission to feel confused."
"I have permission to feel it all."

Repeat any of them as many times as you need until you begin to physically and emotionally experience the shock and denial.

SOMATIC ACTIVITIES
Shock & Denial

Then, repeating the physical movements, begin saying these mantras:

"This was a shocking experience."
"My shock is completely warranted."
"This is hard to fathom."
"Of course it's hard to believe."

Repeat any of them as many times as you need until you begin to physically and emotionally experience the pain & guilt.

Then, repeating the physical movements, begin saying these mantras:

"I have permission to feel this shock for as long as I need to."
"I have permission to feel confused."
"I have permission to feel it all."

Repeat any of them as many times as you need until you begin to physically and emotionally experience the anger.

Slowly invite yourself out of the practice, repeating this for any physical area you identified in your original list, and as many times as you wish throughout the week.

SOMATIC ACTIVITIES
Shock & Denial

REFLECT: I encourage you to reflect on the somatic experience below.

PHASE TWO
Pain & Guilt

DATE:

This week, I'd like you to take some time to journal through the second stage of grief: "Pain and Guilt."

You can do this all at once, more than once, or in chunks throughout the week.

Additionally, I will have you do some somatic (physical) practices related to this journaling exercise, which are below the journaling prompts.

NOTE: Please make sure you are in a safe, quiet, comfortable space (mentally and physically) when beginning this. You can set up a cozy nook in your room, light a candle, or play soft music. Make sure you won't be distracted or interrupted (avoid public places and try to turn your phone off). This practice may bring up a lot physically and emotionally, and it's important to take good care of yourself before, during, and after.

ABOUT
Pain & Guilt

EXPERIENCE

Guilt, shame, regret, and the notion that "I could have done something" is often the next phase. Additionally, some people experience guilt around being a burden to others in their grieving process, feeling their sadness, need for support, or "inability to move on" is cumbersome to their loved ones.

CHALLENGE

Realizing there is nothing to feel guilty over, reducing shame, asking for help.

GOAL

Permission to lean on others, seek support and community, challenge false beliefs about what "I could have done"

JOURNALING PROMPTS
Pain & Guilt

What is the event, experience, or loss I am grieving and working through for this exercise? *Describe it in as much detail as you are able to, recalling the date, weather, where you were, what you heard, smelled...try to incorporate in your journaling a full story that encompasses all the senses surrounding the event/how you learned of the event.*

When I think about this event, is there anything I feel guilty or ashamed about? If so, what thoughts do I have?

When I think about this event, what are my regrets?

Are my regrets warranted? If so, why? If not, where did this story come from?

JOURNALING PROMPTS
Pain & Guilt

What do I wish I could have done or changed?

What does it feel like knowing I can't go back and change anything?
(refer to the feelings wheel here--I want you to get in the habit of
identifying actual emotions rather than thoughts).

Imagine feeling guilt about this event. Where do I feel it in my body?
Do this for regret, shame, or burdensome if those resonate.

JOURNALING PROMPTS
Pain & Guilt

When this event occurred, who did I reach out to for support? What was that experience like? If I didn't, why not?

Who have I processed this event with since? If I haven't, why not?

'

Who could I lean on now to process this with?

Do I think I should be "over this" by now? Why? Where does this idea come from?

JOURNALING PROMPTS
Pain & Guilt

When I still experience pain, regret, or guilt about this event, do I lean on anyone for support? Why or why not?

What do I need to do to release my guilt or the belief that "I could have done something different?"

What do I need to do to give myself permission to lean on others?

SOMATIC ACTIVITIES
Pain & Guilt

IDENTIFY: Once you have moved through the journaling prompts, make a brief list of the places you identified feeling pain, guilt, and regret in your body below:

ACTIVITY: Find a comfortable seated position, and place one hand over the body part you have identified, and another over your heart. You can close your eyes or keep them open.

Gently massage, rub in circles, or use two fingers to "tap" the identified, while repeating these mantras to yourself:

"I feel guilty."
"I feel regret."
"I feel ashamed."
"I feel like a burden."
"I feel pain."
Repeat any of them as many times as you need until you begin to physically and emotionally experience the pain and guilt.

Slowly invite yourself out of the practice, repeating this for any physical area you identified in your original list, and as many times as you wish throughout the week.

SOMATIC ACTIVITIES
Pain & Guilt

Then, repeating the physical movements, begin saying these mantras:

"It's painful to know I had no control."
"It's painful to feel this all on my own."
"Guilt and shame are so painful to feel."

Repeat any of them as many times as you need until you begin to physically and emotionally experience the pain & guilt.

Then, repeating the physical movements, begin saying these mantras:

"I am not a burden."
"I am not responsible for what happened to me."
"This was not my fault."
"It's ok to ask for support while grieving."

Repeat any of them as many times as you need until you begin to physically and emotionally experience the shock and denial.

REFLECT: I encourage you to reflect on the somatic experience below.

ACTION ITEMS
Pain & Guilt

If you identified safe people to process this with, I invite you to reach out to them and share this experience with them. Allow yourself to be seen and held by others as you move through this process.

If you reached out to someone, feel free to reflect below on how that impacted you.

PHASE THREE
Anger & Bargaining

DATE:

This week, I'd like you to take some time to journal through the third stage of grief: "Anger and Bargaining."

You can do this all at once, more than once, or in chunks throughout the week.

You can choose one grief area to focus on, or make multiple entries around different areas in your life you are grieving.

Additionally, I will have you do some somatic (physical) practices related to this journaling exercise, which are below the journaling prompts.

NOTE: Please make sure you are in a safe, quiet, comfortable space (mentally and physically) when beginning this. You can set up a cozy nook in your room, light a candle, or play soft music. Make sure you won't be distracted or interrupted (avoid public places and try to turn your phone off). This practice may bring up a lot physically and emotionally, and it's important to take good care of yourself before, during, and after.

ABOUT
Anger & Bargaining

EXPERIENCE

Anger is often bypassed or displaced in the grief process. Culturally, we don't encourage or teach healthy expression of anger, so we often push anger away, even in our day to day lives. This can show up as self-hatred, distracting, shame around feeling anger at all, lashing out at others, feeling anger towards a higher power, or simply denying that we are angry at all. Bargaining shows up as a means for us to avoid many of the existing and upcoming emotions that we know are painful: if we can change the course of history or the future, maybe we won't have to feel so angry, sad, or confused. We may try to bargain with a higher power, with an ex if the loss is a relationship, or with ourselves.

CHALLENGE

Expressing anger, feeling anger, directing anger in appropriate spaces.

GOAL

Healthy expression of anger, acceptance and validation of anger, allowance for full range of emotional expression, physical practices of releasing anger.

JOURNALING PROMPTS
Anger & Bargaining

What is the event, experience, or loss I am grieving and working through for this exercise? *Describe it in as much detail as you are able to, recalling the date, weather, where you were, what you heard, smelled...try to incorporate in your journaling a full story that encompasses all the senses surrounding the event/how you learned of the event.*

When I think about this event, what do I feel angry about?

When I think about this event, what do I wish I could change?

JOURNALING PROMPTS
Anger & Bargaining

How have I tried to bargain or change the outcome of this situation?

Who am I angry at? *List everyone (even if you are one of them) and write what you are angry at them for and why. Remember, this doesn't mean you don't love or like them--it's ok to be angry at someone, and we can feel anger towards others (or ourselves) and still love them.*

When I think about my anger, what are the specific anger-related emotions that I feel? *(Use a feelings wheel here to identify specific anger emotions)*

JOURNALING PROMPTS
Anger & Bargaining

Imagine feeling anger about this event. Where do you feel it in your body?

Imagine feeling anger toward the person/people related to this event. Where do you feel it in your body?

When this event occurred, did I express my anger? If so how? If not, what did I do with my anger? Why didn't I express it?

If I still haven't expressed my anger, why not?

SOMATIC ACTIVITIES
Anger & Bargaining

IDENTIFY: Once you have moved through the journaling prompts, make a brief list of the places you identified feeling anger in your body below:

ACTIVITY: Find a comfortable seated position, and place one hand over the body part you have identified, and another over your heart. You can close your eyes or keep them open.

Gently massage, rub in circles, or use two fingers to "tap" the identified, while repeating these mantras to yourself:

"I feel angry."
"I feel anger."
"I feel furious."

Include any other emotions you identified in the journaling prompts above.
Repeat any of them as many times as you need until you begin to physically and emotionally experience the anger.

Slowly invite yourself out of the practice, repeating this for any physical area you identified in your original list, and as many times as you wish throughout the week.

SOMATIC ACTIVITIES
Anger & Bargaining

Then, repeating the physical movements, begin saying these mantras:

"It's painful to have this anger and not be able to express it."
"I hurt myself by not expressing my anger."
"I betray myself by not honoring my anger."

Repeat any of them as many times as you need until you begin to physically and emotionally experience the pain & guilt.

Then, repeating the physical movements, begin saying these mantras:

"Anger does not make me a bad person."
"I have the right to feel and express my anger."
"It is healthy for me to express anger."
"I can feel anger and it won't take control of me."

Repeat any of them as many times as you need until you begin to physically and emotionally experience the anger.

SOMATIC ACTIVITIES
Anger & Bargaining

REFLECT: I encourage you to reflect on the somatic experience below.

ACTION ITEMS
Anger & Bargaining

Anger is a difficult emotion for many of us to express, as it makes us feel like we ourselves are suddenly an "angry person."

Our emotions do not make us who we are--and *no emotion has more power over another.*

I invite you to write mantras around normalizing anger, and equalizing it in context of all other feelings below.

PHASE FOUR
Depression & Sorrow

DATE:

This week, I'd like you to take some time to journal through the fourth stage of grief: "Depression & Sorrow."

You can do this all at once, more than once, or in chunks throughout the week.

Additionally, I will invite you to do some somatic (physical) practices related to this journaling exercise, which are below the journaling prompts.

NOTE: Please make sure you are in a safe, quiet, comfortable space (mentally and physically) when beginning this. You can set up a cozy nook in your room, light a candle, or play soft music. Make sure you won't be distracted or interrupted (avoid public places and try to turn your phone off). This practice may bring up a lot physically and emotionally, and it's important to take good care of yourself before, during, and after.

ABOUT
Depression & Sorrow

EXPERIENCE

When bargaining ends, when denial fades, and when we've expressed our anger and pain, we are left with the deep and utter sorrow of our loss. This phase is the most potent, and often the most difficult to come out of.

CHALLENGE

Finding hope, moving from depression to the upward turn, getting daily tasks done.

GOAL

Feel the sorrow, truly mourn, find rituals, and make meaning from the sadness and sorrow.

JOURNALING PROMPTS
Depression & Sorrow

What is the event, experience, or loss I am grieving and working through for this exercise? *Describe it in as much detail as you are able to, recalling the date, weather, where you were, what you heard, smelled...try to incorporate in your journaling a full story that encompasses all the senses surrounding the event/how you learned of the event.*

When I think about this event, what do I feel sad about?

When I think about this event, what do I ruminate or get stuck on?

How have I let myself feel sorrow over this loss? *Have I let myself feel sorrow?*

JOURNALING PROMPTS
Depression & Sorrow

What or who do I miss? What or who do I long for?

When I think about my sadness and sorrow, what are the specific sad-related emotions that I feel? *(Use a feelings wheel here to identify specific sad emotions)*

Imagine feeling sorrow about this loss. Where do you feel it in your body?

JOURNALING PROMPTS
Depression & Sorrow

Imagine feeling depressed about this loss. Where do you feel it in your body?

When this event occurred, did I express my sorrow? If so how? If not, what did I do with my sadness? Why didn't I express it?

If I still haven't expressed my sorrow, why not?

SOMATIC ACTIVITIES
Depression & Sorrow

IDENTIFY: Once you have moved through the journaling prompts, make a brief list of the places you identified feeling shock and denial in your body below:

ACTIVITY: Find a comfortable seated position, and place one hand over the body part you have identified, and another over your heart. You can close your eyes or keep them open.

Gently massage, rub in circles, or use two fingers to "tap" the identified, while repeating these mantras to yourself:

"I feel depressed."
"I feel sad."
"I feel sorrow."

Include any other emotions you identified in the journaling prompts above.

Repeat any of them as many times as you need until you begin to physically and emotionally experience the depression & sorrow.

SOMATIC ACTIVITIES
Depression & Sorrow

Then, repeating the physical movements, begin saying these mantras:

"This is such a sad thing that happened."
"I hold onto the past when I do not let myself mourn."
"I am free to be sad and can allow it to come out."

Repeat any of them as many times as you need until you begin to physically and emotionally experience the pain & guilt.

Then, repeating the physical movements, begin saying these mantras:

"I have the right to feel deeply saddened by this loss."
"I can feel my sadness as long as I need to."
"It is normal to feel depressed in the wake of a loss like mine."
"I can feel sad and still find myself in joy again."

Repeat any of them as many times as you need until you begin to physically and emotionally experience the anger.

Slowly invite yourself out of the practice, repeating this for any physical area you identified in your original list, and as many times as you wish throughout the week.

SOMATIC ACTIVITIES
Depression & Sorrow

REFLECT: I encourage you to reflect on the somatic experience below.

ACTION ITEMS
Depression & Sorrow

Sorrow is a difficult emotion for many of us to recover from: it is usually a *feeling that develops into a mood,* and *a mood that lasts a long time* and can *turn into a temperament.*

Often, we can get stuck in this phase because we equate sorrow and depression to ongoing, lifelong temperaments rather than feelings that rise and fall just like any other. *(please know I am not discounting the real experience of chronic or clinical depression.)*

How can you feel depressed about this loss *without it meaning you are depressed?* How can you feel and express sorrow and *still know there is joy on the horizon?*

Who can you talk to about this concept?

PHASE FIVE
The Upward Turn

DATE:

This week, I'd like you to take some time to journal through the fifth stage of grief: "The Upward Turn."

You can do this all at once, more than once, or in chunks throughout the week.

Additionally, I will invite you to do some somatic (physical) practices related to this journaling exercise, which are below the journaling prompts.

NOTE: Please make sure you are in a safe, quiet, comfortable space (mentally and physically) when beginning this. You can set up a cozy nook in your room, light a candle, or play soft music. Make sure you won't be distracted or interrupted (avoid public places and try to turn your phone off). This practice may bring up a lot physically and emotionally, and it's important to take good care of yourself before, during, and after.

ABOUT
The Upward Turn

EXPERIENCE

Over time, the intensity of the depression, anger, bargaining, denial, and guilt fade and come less often. We may start to notice ourselves enjoying activities again, thinking less about the loss, or having a sense of hope or possibility.

CHALLENGE

Grace when old stages are revisited during this time, pacing oneself, not doing too much all at once.

GOAL

Daily rituals, returning to work and social life, seeking hope.

JOURNALING PROMPTS
The Upward Turn

What is the event, experience, or loss I am grieving and working through for this exercise? *Describe it in as much detail as you are able to, recalling the date, weather, where you were, what you heard, smelled...try to incorporate in your journaling a full story that encompasses all the senses surrounding the event/how you learned of the event.*

When I think about the future, how does this event fit in?

What positivity has occurred as an outcome of this loss?

How have I noticed a shift in my mood since grieving this loss?

JOURNALING PROMPTS
The Upward Turn

What do I experience hope for?

What is possible now that I have grieved this loss?

Imagine feeling hope in the wake of this loss. Where do you feel it in your body?

Imagine feeling optimism, knowing you have moved through this grieving process. Where do you feel it in your body?

Imagine that a day comes in the future when you revisit sorrow, anger, bargaining, or shock around this event. What words of wisdom can you impart on your future self?

SOMATIC ACTIVITIES
The Upward Turn

IDENTIFY: Once you have moved through the journaling prompts, make a brief list of the places you identified feeling shock and denial in your body below:

ACTIVITY: Find a comfortable seated position, and place one hand over the body part you have identified, and another over your heart. You can close your eyes or keep them open.

Gently massage, rub in circles, or use two fingers to "tap" the identified, while repeating these mantras to yourself:

"I feel hopeful."
"I feel optimistic."

Include any other emotions you identified in the journaling prompts above.

Repeat any of them as many times as you need until you begin to physically and emotionally experience the hope and optimism.

SOMATIC ACTIVITIES
The Upward Turn

Then, repeating the physical movements, begin saying these mantras:

"I have hope for the future."
"I see possibility and opportunity."
"I am free to be optimistic and still honor the past."

Repeat any of them as many times as you need until you begin to physically and emotionally experience the hope and optimism.

Then, repeating the physical movements, begin saying these mantras:

"I have the right to feel hopeful."
"If I feel sad again, it does not tae away from the work I have done."
"It is normal to feel hopeful after moving through grief."
"I have permission to feel joy again."

Repeat any of them as many times as you need until you begin to physically and emotionally experience the optimism and hope.

Slowly invite yourself out of the practice, repeating this for any physical area you identified in your original list, and as many times as you wish throughout the week.

SOMATIC ACTIVITIES
The Upward Turn

REFLECT: I encourage you to reflect on the somatic experience below.

ACTION ITEMS
The Upward Turn

Often, we can become inflated or "high" in this newfound hope.
Other times, we return to guilt, feeling shame for having joy when there is such a loss behind us.

All of this is normal--take stock of your emotional state in this hopefulness.

Simply notice your reaction: do you attach to the optimism and let it take you high high up? Or, do you fear it/avoid it out of guilt or shame?

Become mindful and self-compassionate for your response, and allow what comes up to come up, and use this space during the week to non-judgmentally note your observations.

PHASE SIX
Reconstruction &
Working Through

DATE:

This week, I'd like you to take some time to journal through the sixth stage of grief: "Reconstruction & Working Through."

You can do this all at once, more than once, or in chunks throughout the week.

Additionally, I will invite you to do some somatic (physical) practices related to this journaling exercise, which are below the journaling prompts.

NOTE: Please make sure you are in a safe, quiet, comfortable space (mentally and physically) when beginning this. You can set up a cozy nook in your room, light a candle, or play soft music. Make sure you won't be distracted or interrupted (avoid public places and try to turn your phone off). This practice may bring up a lot physically and emotionally, and it's important to take good care of yourself before, during, and after.

ABOUT
Reconstruction & Working Through

EXPERIENCE

In this phase, we are able to reflect on the loss and integrate it into our reality and the narrative of our history. We begin to rebuild our lives in the absence of the loss, moving forward with our daily tasks, work, relationships, and interests.

CHALLENGE

Grace when old stages are revisited during this time, wondering how to "do this alone," navigating self-doubt.

GOAL

Tell your story, make meaning, reflect on what was learned.

JOURNALING PROMPTS
Reconstruction & Working Through

What is the event, experience, or loss I am grieving and working through for this exercise? *Describe it in as much detail as you are able to, recalling the date, weather, where you were, what you heard, smelled...try to incorporate in your journaling a full story that encompasses all the senses surrounding the event/how you learned of the event.*

What have I learned from this loss?

What have I learned from this grief experience?

JOURNALING PROMPTS
Reconstruction & Working Through

How does this fit into the story of my life?

What does life look like for me now?

How can I be kind to myself if I fall back into old phases of grief?

JOURNALING PROMPTS
Reconstruction & Working Through

Imagine feeling one of the old phases again at some point. Which emotions do I anticipate feeling about returning to old phases?

Where do I feel the above feelings in my body?

How can I make meaning of this experience?

How can I tell my story, create something, or share so that others can learn from this?

ACTION ITEMS
Reconstruction & Working Through

(This phase does not require Somatic Activities)

List as many creative outlets you can think of to support you in sharing your story--whether publicly or privately. These are mechanisms to share the full narrative of this story, whether in the context of your life or as a standalone experience.

What is one activity above you can engage in this week as a means to express your grief story holistically?

PHASE SEVEN
Acceptance & Hope

DATE:

This week, I'd like you to take some time to journal through the seventh stage of grief: "Acceptance & Hope."

You can do this all at once, more than once, or in chunks throughout the week.

Additionally, I will invite you to do some somatic (physical) practices related to this journaling exercise, which are below the journaling prompts.

NOTE: Please make sure you are in a safe, quiet, comfortable space (mentally and physically) when beginning this. You can set up a cozy nook in your room, light a candle, or play soft music. Make sure you won't be distracted or interrupted (avoid public places and try to turn your phone off). This practice may bring up a lot physically and emotionally, and it's important to take good care of yourself before, during, and after.

ABOUT
Acceptance & Hope

EXPERIENCE

Hope and acceptance may visit throughout the entire grief process. These feelings grow stronger in time, and ultimately outweigh the experience of depression, denial, guilt, or anger that may continue to arise from time to time.

CHALLENGE

Grace when old stages are revisited during this time, navigating other people's narratives of your recovery.

GOAL

Feeling confident and secure in your grief process, seeing the past through a lens of gratitude and peace, seeing the future through a lens of hope and optimism, resilience-building.

JOURNALING PROMPTS
Acceptance & Hope

What is the event, experience, or loss I am grieving and working through for this exercise? *Describe it in as much detail as you are able to, recalling the date, weather, where you were, what you heard, smelled...try to incorporate in your journaling a full story that encompasses all the senses surrounding the event/how you learned of the event.*

What have I accepted about this loss or event?

What have I still not accepted, or struggle to accept?

JOURNALING PROMPTS
Acceptance & Hope

What would fully accepting this loss as reality allow me to do?

What am I hopeful for when I think about how this event has impacted me?

How can I be kind to myself if I fall back into old phases of grief?

JOURNALING PROMPTS
Acceptance & Hope

Where do I feel acceptance in my body?

Where do I feel hope in my body?

If I find myself back in a space of un-acceptance or denial, how can I be compassionate to myself?

SOMATIC ACTIVITIES
Acceptance & Hope

IDENTIFY: Once you have moved through the journaling prompts, make a brief list of the places you identified feeling shock and denial in your body below:

ACTIVITY: Find a comfortable seated position, and place one hand over the body part you have identified, and another over your heart. You can close your eyes or keep them open.

Gently massage, rub in circles, or use two fingers to "tap" the identified, while repeating these mantras to yourself:

"I feel hopeful."
"I feel acceptance."

Include any other emotions you identified in the journaling prompts above.

Repeat any of them as many times as you need until you begin to physically and emotionally experience the hope and acceptance.

SOMATIC ACTIVITIES
Acceptance & Hope

Then, repeating the physical movements, begin saying these mantras:

"I have hope for the future."
"I see possibility and opportunity."
"I am free to be optimistic and still honor the past."

Repeat any of them as many times as you need until you begin to physically and emotionally experience the hope and optimism.

Then, repeating the physical movements, begin saying these mantras:

"I have the right to feel hopeful."
"If I feel sad again, it does not tae away from the work I have done."
"It is normal to feel hopeful after moving through grief."
"I have permission to feel joy again."

Repeat any of them as many times as you need until you begin to physically and emotionally experience the optimism and hope.

Slowly invite yourself out of the practice, repeating this for any physical area you identified in your original list, and as many times as you wish throughout the week.

SOMATIC ACTIVITIES
Acceptance & Hope

REFLECT: I encourage you to reflect on the somatic experience below.

ACTION ITEMS
Acceptance & Hope

Make a list of mantras that have to do with acceptance, surrender, and letting go.

What is one hope you have for yourself as a result of this event?

How can you embody this hope, either in an action or activity?

FINAL REFLECTION

Take a few minutes to reflect back on the last 7 weeks. What have you learned about your grief?

What have you discovered about your resilience?

How can you continue to honor your grief, your loss, and how you've grown and overcome?

Feelings Wheel

the outermost feelings are heightened, magnified, or specific versions of their core emotion

start by asking yourself:

"what am I feeling in this moment?"

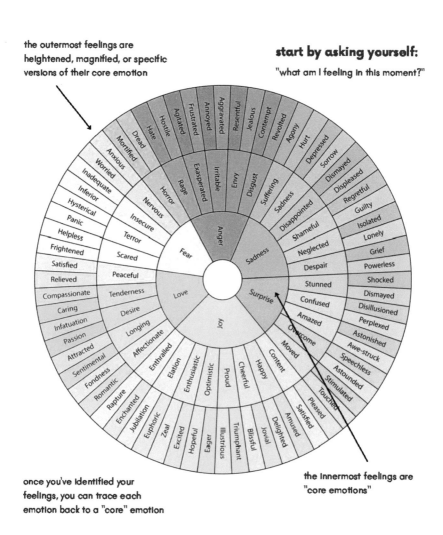

once you've identified your feelings, you can trace each emotion back to a "core" emotion

the innermost feelings are "core emotions"

Made in United States
Cleveland, OH
12 November 2024

10630900R00043